diane wakoski

GREED

parts 3 and 4

los angeles
black sparrow press
1969

Greed, Parts I & II is now available in
Diane Wakoski's book *The Magellanic Clouds.*

GREED

PART III

The Greed That Is Not Greed

(a poem with no universals, with very personal histories

& exploring a subject mentioned by Robert Kelly)

RARELY do I let myself
        write, mentioning real names of places.
        But in discussing the matter of greed,
        I, always slightly overweight according to Vogue standards,
        and living in the richest country in the world,
        would not be fairly using the material at hand
        were I not to speak of my experiences.
        Robert Kelly is overweight.
        I do not believe that it is greed that makes him eat
        too much,
        but hunger.
        He probably does not eat much more than George Washington
        who was about the same height (6′ 4″),
        but his body makes fat out of the food.
        In my original concept of greed,
        I judged anything in excess to be a result of greed.
        Kelly pointed out that this is not strictly
        true.
        Greed is motivated by deprivation & resultant pettiness.
        Many things done in excess by one man's standard
        are only the norm
        by another's.
        If I were to require a 350 pound man to eat my daily diet,
        I would starve him.
        And once you accept this,
        you accept the concept of the variable norm.
        The Variable Norm.
        Once it is variable
        who is to say it is a standard any longer?

Over a period of years
    having been a somewhat social person
    I have definitely seen many acts of greed.
    An act out of a desire of excess
    that leads to a man's debasement
    is greed.
    Having 2 wives
    if it divides your house
    your mind
    or your loyalties
    is an act of greed. But generosity
    would not necessarily
    have a better result. The greed, perhaps,
    is not in having 2 women
    but in having 2 who cannot live in the same house with peace
    or 2 whom you do not love equally, thus giving hurt to one,
    or 2 because of habit or convenience,
    not because 1 will not be enough,
    or 2 because you cannot tell one to go away.

But supply and demand are vicious forces,
    making a man wallow when there is plenty
    and cry when there's not enough.
    The ungreedy eats the same every day,
    saving the plenty to augment the sparse.
    In any area where you've conquered supply and demand
    you've conquered greed.
    For instance, Diane, the wife of the Hawk's Well Head,
    who told me she'd never pay $30 for a dress
    because whether she were rich or poor, it seemed like
    the wrong price.
    Some of the richest men
    walk around from year to year
    with a fixed idea of how much something should cost.
    And with that stability
    they are seldom at the mercy
    of their fortunes.
    In matters of money
    at least
    they have no greed.

Every time I think of greed,
       I think of the bitterness it causes,
       of what it takes away from others,
       how it destroys some balance
       that we are all trying to set up.
       Putting one thing above all others
       usually results in some form of greed.
       It is true that we usually look at our one obsession in life
       as a right, because we are willing to
       sacrifice other parts of our life for it;
       but there is no such thing as self-sacrifice
       without hurting others.
       Only a complete hermit and orphan can say
       that by following his greedy obsession to be alone
       he is hurting or depriving no one.
       We are social creatures;
       all our actions reflect back to others.

Rarely do I express my hostilities
     without also defending the person
     I feel anger towards.
     Sometimes defending him more than
     he would himself.
     I feel that to express anger
     without also giving mitigating circumstances
     or explanations
     is a greed. And that greed destroys
     the greedy.
     My anger with Carol Bergé
     that beautiful black orchid of the Chelsea
     for her poison pen letter to me
     in December 1967 telling me that I am too aggressive (Blaming it,
     of course, on some poor constellation in the sky which happened
     to harbor the sun when I was born)
     has made me so angry
     that I constantly find it necessary to say nice things about her
     even when no one else wants to.
     It is a choice of greeds, sometimes.
     When I would rather like everyone than hate anyone.
     But there is a greed which is not greed. It is the desire to have,
     to know, to experience, be,
     everything,
     so that you can share it, possess it with the world.
     Desire
     for the purpose of control or
     excluding others
     or of total ownership
     is greed
     whether motivated out of extreme need

or sheer petulence.
The effect can only debase the spirit.
Clayton Eshleman is often accused of being greedy for power.
He edits a literary magazine;
he has deep political commitments;
he left his wife in a very unsympathetic manner
because of a desire to shape his life differently than he could living
in her presence.
He, like Kelly, is not greedy for power.
He suffers from the greed which is not greed.
The greed to know everything,
to be everything,
to say everything.
But it is a desire to be complete with the world
and there accompanies it
a willingness to share all,
to include all,
to give all.
          Provided he/they are given all.
That demand
                to be given all
yes, it is a greed.
But a greed that in the long run
is not
greed;
perhaps if sustained long enough,
carried far enough
becomes
greatness.

Telling Ted Berrigan,
       as a point of honor or integrity
       (and beware of the users of that last word,
       the breeding of self-righteousness)
       that I don't like his poems,
       is an act of greed on my part.
       His life is as honest as anyone's.
       His poems are as important to him
       as mine are to me.
       He has a different style
       a different way of life
       a different set of values
       but whereas I don't like his poems any less
       than I like the poems of lots of other poets,
       I don't like the way he treats his wife,
       and so I put him down publicly.
       It is a sign of rotten moral greed
       to be so frugal with approval.
       The greed of a man who can genuinely like everyone,
       maybe just because they're human beings,
       is the greed that is not greed.
       Do not confuse this with wanting everyone to like you.

Kelly has a talent of giving
that, even with the best of intentions,
few others could show.
Perhaps it is that he has the language
to communicate to everyone.
Most of my friends are good people
as well as good poets
in my judgment.
None of them are greed-less
but most are intelligent
and know what their greed is
and how to compensate for it.
Jerome Rothenberg is greedy for peace & harmony
having lived all the centuries of the Jew's persecution
in his mind.
David Antin is greedy for authority on every subject.
Jackson MacLow is greedy to write every poem at least once, try
every idea.
Armand Schwerner to unite science and art.
Rochelle Owens to say every swear word and have every erotic
experience.
Jack Anderson to make everything unusual.
Paul Blackburn to be able to talk to anyone, on any level, &
communicate.

Everyone has his own greed
       and suffers from it. It stops being greed
       when it is understood
       and compensated for. When it leads to
       a greater product
       a fullness
       otherwise not there.
       The greed that is not greed
       benefits others,
       even while destroying some part of you.

Lonely poets. We need to be alone to think.
       Our hallucinations creep up on us
       and scare us into company. We talk.
       We tell everything we dreamed or felt,
       what we saw in the dark,
       the stone breathing,
       the trees pulling our hair.

Lying poets. Making up stories
       to exonerate ourselves.
       to hide the greed.
       It is not necessary.

Young children don't hide their needs.
They don't hide desire either.
The greed that is not greed
goes one step beyond the scratch in the phonograph record,
the spot that repeats over & over,
cannot get beyond itself.
The man who acknowledges his ill
that he needs more than the norm or more than others allow
and who takes it, in the face of all accusations,
but gives it back with interest.
He is the great man.   The man who
takes greed beyond greed.

GREED

PART IV

Intruders

This child is born
just having sloughed off his tail
into some blood stream
after nine months of tasting salt
and feeling warm water
touch his cheeks;
sometimes he drops feet first into the world
ready to run,
but usually head first
battering a path with his skull.

How many of us are born
as intruders,
unwanted nuisances,
ugly noisy holes
to be plugged?

Anyone who has entered as an intruder,
whose small unshod feet
walked only on floors that belonged to others,
whose hands tried to touch objects
which always belonged to others and were snatched away,
whose very words or cries were impositions
on someone else's place or time;
anyone of us who spent his first years
as an intruder
will spend his life trying to overcome
the feeling
that nothing belonged to him;
we were welcome no place,
there was nothing we could do that was not grudgingly tolerated;
we took up space that was not ours,
time that did not belong to us,

energy that could have been used more happily elsewhere,
money that could have been spent on something else,
food that no one wanted to give us,
even the affection or love that came,
perhaps just for our small helplessness,
was intended for someone else
and spilled accidentally
like a bottle of ink
under a dragging sleeve,
on us.

The intruders,
we,
who had nothing to give,
whose existence was interpreted as a burden,
pennies that would not go in a nickel slot,
oil on water.

Is it any wonder that we wind ourselves in thick shells
(like turtles)
of possessions,
deeds,
documents of ownership,
titles to right of way,
licenses giving us legal rights,
diplomas,
credentials?
We try to secure ourselves against loss
of love,
of houses,
of food,
of jobs,
of honor,
of dignity,
of identity.
We become landlords of the emotions.

Being a Landlord of the Emotions

Breaking off inside me
is a thin narrow bone of contention
        /called a poet/
a star or Baltimore oriole
gummed-sticker from a good piano lesson,
a cactus rose
whose succulent flat face,
as a lettuce,
or Mexican girl
in embroidered white blouse
bares its small teeth
in a smile.

This accident,
this river
of feelings,
making me need a spool of gold jewelers' wire
to tie down my fluttering heart,
the one that teeters
uneasily in high heels,
a heart making its first appearance.

What happened?
How was I born to worry so much
about the possibilities
of loneliness?

I think I am a man who worships
his own prisons;
why else would I be so concerned about rings,
deeds,
ownership?
I am a landlord, I think,

of the emotions,
just trying to collect my rents,
regularly.

You have what you were born with. No more.
How I have fought that rule;
and worshipped it.

The pain of life.
We are born
as diamonds
having to endure the world's
cutting us into shape
or we remain
undiscovered
like dirty chunks of rock.

I speak again
here
of myself,
not because I am different from you.
We were,
I think,
all intruders
to some measure
and try to create in our adult lives
a sense of mastery,
over our surroundings: the world no longer will just
"tolerate" us —
we will see to that.
We will be the owners,
the possessors,
the ones who must be petitioned, the landlords.

And it is understandable,
real,

a way of taking the past and thrusting it in a closet,
getting it out of sight;
but it breeds a kind of greed
that in its very rationality
can overtake us,
become impossible to purge. We can excuse it
too easily, can condone it,
can even use it as an excuse
to help other people.
But as it becomes insulated with reason and
understanding,
it grows and grows. The greater this need of possession,
of security, of insulation from the past,
the greater significance does that past itself
obtain.
You never lose the sense of being an intruder.
And what is more,
you cast everyone in your life into that role —
the intruder who's using your possessions,
the intruder who's taking up your time,
the intruder who's accidentally stealing your affections.

The Turtle

The turtle swims slowly,
leisurely.
On the volcanic ashland of the Galapagos
where the turtles weigh 200 pounds;
you could see one
move slowly
dragging trails to the middle of an island
where he finds fresh spring water;
you might see one pushing
for hours
against a deep rock
or a tree trunk
because the object was in his way
and it never occurred to him
to go around,
never occurred either
that he could not push over the object
if he just kept pushing
even if it took several
days.

The turtle carries everything he needs
with him,
except food and water;
he is a complete man of possessions;
no one ever intrudes on his house.
Not until death.
Stubborn,
slow,
unbelieving that the world
could defy him,
he is a survivor.
A creature so weak,
so vulnerable,
but somehow
impervious.

If only life left us with metaphors.
But we are lucky if life
leaves us
with life.

How can we condemn
that greed then
which manifests itself as a survival force,
a desire to insulate ourselves
from onslaught,
to possess those things which keep us daily
from the edge of despair?
Only because there is no way to do it
without robbing our lives
of their reality.
Surrounded by possessions,
we become once removed from life.
Then life becomes once removed from us.
As if to destroy your car
is to destroy a piece of you;
to take away your house
is to take away the years of you that lived in it;
to take away your money
is to take away the character that earned it;
to leave you,
saying
maybe I couldn't do it again;
to take away your clothes
is to take away your image
as the world sees you;
to take away your jewels
is to remove your beauty.

All life then
but a little spark
that keeps the heart going back and forth
between the starting and finishing lines.
And you remove one possession at a time;
thus removing you.

How can we blame
a man for his greed, his desire
to own things that represent himself
and then to so value them
that the self is forgotten
as a little *a priori* consideration,
a guilty match
that started the whole Chicago fire.

But we are authors,
all of us,
concerned with beginning,
with making,
with sources and substance. And those possessions,
the objects of our desire for security
are results,
not causes,
in our lives. When we too much honor
them, we start weakening ourselves
and fear of loss
becomes even greater than the desire
for life.
A pistol shot in the head
when the '29 market crashes.
A slashed wrist
when the jewels are taken by popular revolt.
An alcoholic condition
when the house goes back to the bank.
The greed for possessions:
fear that we'll be left only with ourselves,
become intruders,
once more,
living in a world
that finds us a burden.
Greed.
Who cannot say it is not a survival trait?
Look how it keeps the evil alive;
look how early
good men die.

And I,
the author of all this,
the landlord of the emotions I call myself earlier,
giving up so much,
but wanting so much more.

How can I sign myself?
Other than as
another greedy man?
How can I sign myself,
sitting in someone else's chair,
fearing the opposite of this man
        even the world
fearing to buy my own chair?

Is there any place
that could take me beyond these concerns?

Yes.
An answer
could be in your hand,
your face,
your mustache
brushing my lips. My greedy desire
is not to possess you,
only to love you,
just to touch you,
old man,
Galapagos turtle,
intruder.
You,
landlord
of my heart.

January 22, 1969

38

Printed September 1969 in Santa Barbara by
Noel Young for the Black Sparrow Press.
Design by Barbara Martin. This book is
published in three editions: 300 numbered
copies sewn in paper wrappers signed by
the poet; 150 numbered copies handbound
in boards by Earle Gray signed by the poet;
& 250 unsigned copies stapled in paper wrappers.